Painless Acts

Painless Acts

Published by The Conrad Press in the United Kingdom 2020

Tel: +44(0)1227 472 874
www.theconradpress.com
info@theconradpress.com

ISBN 978-1-913567-50-7

Copyright © Trevor Kennett, 2020 www.trevorkennett.com

The moral right of Trevor Kennett to be identified as author of this work has been asserted in accordance with the Copyright, Designs and Patents Act 1988.

All rights reserved.

Typesetting and Cover Design by: Charlotte Mouncey, www.bookstyle.co.uk

The Conrad Press logo was designed by Maria Priestley.

Printed and bound in Great Britain by Clays Ltd, Elcograf S.p.A.

Painless Acts

Trevor Kennett

This television drama is dedicated to all those people and organisations who have inspired me during my working life.

AUTHOR'S NOTE

Before you begin to read this television screenplay, I would like to tell you a little bit about my background and working life that has inspired this story.

I started my career in the late 1970s as a police cadet, which informed my early working days in public life, but not as I was expecting. My cadet days were filled with virtually no police work whatsoever, which was a bit of a shock to me I can tell you. Instead my time was filled with glorious summer days, swimming, canoeing, rock climbing and my passion at the time: cross-country running. Hardly the training for a budding Sherlock Holmes who is someone I have always longed to be.

This soon ended abruptly when I became eighteen and a half and had to join the regular force. In the early 1980s as a uniformed constable things became sometimes weird or funny, but more often life-changing, with harrowing incidents that shaped my young adult life. While my friends were worrying about girls and motorbikes, I was on a deployment to the Coroner's office getting to grips with my first of many post-mortems.

When I left the police, I developed my working life around being a qualified and accredited investigator in the corporate world. This taught me the value and importance of staying impartial and that good casework is the key to success, along with having some actual evidence and a massive sense of humour.

That said, I have always had a passion for crime scene management, which started, like most people watching classic TV crime dramas, like *The Sweeney* and *Crown Court*. I developed that love affair over a number of years to finally qualify in forensic science. My perseverance paid off with specialisms in surveillance and trace evidence.

I have also been lucky enough to work in a number of Government lead crime task forces, culminating in recognition by the Prime Minister, no less, as an expert practitioner and ambassador in anti-social behaviour, a subject that can affect us all and which plays a minor part in this story.

I hope you enjoy my story, which is about handling our demons and of course painless acts of murder.

PAINLESS ACTS

1979 Inner City in the South East of England.

EXT: RESIDENTIAL STREET - PAST - NIGHT

1970s-styled council estate, parked cars and front doors. A house with all of the lights on and loud punk music playing with a few young people outside drinking, smoking and laughing.

INT: 1970s-STYLE COUNCIL HOUSE - NIGHT

In the kitchen a party is in full swing. 70s punk music is booming out and there are a lot of young people in the kitchen getting drinks talking/laughing and having a good time.

Moving through the house watching party scenes; young party goers in various party scenes, dancing, kissing, drinking, smoking and chatting loudly. The view moves through the house and up the stairs. A couple is on the stairs kissing.

INT: UPSTAIRS LANDING

A few young couples are standing on the landing smoking, drinking and either chatting or kissing.

A young male around eighteen looks up from a girl he is kissing and smiles.

>   YOUNG MALE
>   All right how's it going, you OK?

The young male nods and continues smiling in recognition, the female he is kissing looks annoyed and pulls his face back towards her, travel continues past the couple and up to a bedroom door.

The young male calls out.

>   YOUNG MALE
>   I wouldn't go in there matey.
>   Taff has just shagged Nancy on your bed.
>   Think she is fucked out of her head on Cinzano Rosso.
>   Very, very messy.

Continues to the bedroom door.

INT: BEDROOM

Bedroom door opens and the view is through the door into the bedroom and the door shuts behind.

The bedroom is dark but is lit by an orange streetlight shining through the window as the curtains are not drawn. Punk music can still be heard from downstairs but muted. Looks around a 70s-style bedroom that has basic furniture and a single bed. Nancy is lying on the bed semi-naked and is half asleep/semi-conscious/drunk but mumbling to herself.

The person looks down at the girl and a knife blade can be seen shining in the orange light of the room being held by an unknown person.

INT: KITCHEN

Party in full swing with party goers having a good time, the Sex Pistols, Pretty Vacant is being played with people jumping up and down pogoing, the music is very loud.

INT: BEDROOM

Back to a view of the knife blade, Sex Pistols can be heard from downstairs, the knife is slowly dragged across the girl's stomach in the sign of a cross.

> PERSON NOT SEEN
> As my dear old mother would say you're a harlot,
> hear the word of the Lord, bitch.

EXT: OUTSIDE OF HOUSE – PAST – NIGHT

Group of party goers standing outside of the council house, music blaring, they are shouting, drinking and smoking and the party and their behaviour is getting louder and out of hand... music booming.

INT: BEDROOM

Unseen person holds the point of the blade to Nancy's stomach, and then pulls the knife away as someone bangs on the bedroom door loudly. Male shouting from outside.

                    YOUNG MALE
            Hey, hey you two all right in there,
                  want some company?

Nancy stirs and speaks in a drunken slur.

                       NANCY
            Bastard Taff… dickhead… shagged me.

INT: LIVING ROOM

Party is getting louder and the tension is building, music (Sex Pistols, Pretty Vacant) is pounding, two males start fighting and shouting in the living room.

INT: BEDROOM

Nancy rolls over and is sick in a waste bin by the bed.

END

CREDIT SEQUENCE:

EXT: MODERN OFFICE BUILDING - CITY POLICE OFFICE - PRESENT - DAY

INT: LARGE OPEN SPACE POLICE OFFICE - DAY

Police officers sitting at desks in front of computers, usual busy office scene, telephones ringing, people moving about the office.

Mid-fifties attractive women, Samantha Blaketon is sitting at her desk, typing and looking at her computer talking to a colleague, Matthew Ash who is sitting opposite, and in his late-30s.

SAMANTHA BLAKETON
Look this is really weird right, I'm telling you there was a Post-It note on my screen when I came into work this morning and it had a name written on it. Nancy Williams, then it said Sam check her out, she was my first victim. Weird, right, Matt you listening to me I've a feeling this may be really important.

Samantha is pulling information up on her screen, Matthew is nodding typing away and ignoring her.

SAMANTHA
Then I thought wait, this is a wind up right, is this Matt you bugger, then I thought no this could be for real?

Matthew looking up from his computer.

MATTHEW

Honestly, Sam I haven't got a clue what you are going on about it's not me promise, never heard of her, and I haven't got the time as I am doing your, sorry our work, big report in today, remember?

SAMANTHA

You know you are better with the case figures than me Matt, like I said this is really weird. I started looking for this Nancy Williams and found absolutely nothing in our files, she not known to us, she is not in any youth gang, not a shoplifter not even been causing a nuisance around the local neighbourhoods? I just didn't get it, I was thinking bloody waste of time, then I checked the Police National Database and boom there she was in Major Crime… look.

MATTHEW

If she's not causing any anti-social behaviour, then what has she got to do with us in the Community Safety Unit? You know we are only supposed to be looking at minor crime cases and you shouldn't be poking around in the Police National Database without authorisation from DI Walcott, heard of a thing called audit, have you? You know what Professional Standards will do to you, never mind the boss. Anyway you asked the boss if it was her who left the post-it?

SAMANTHA
Not her handwriting, you don't understand,
Matt, I thought it was a wind up, but it's not,
I'm telling you, now get off your backside
and come look at this?

Matt gets up from his desk and walks over to Sam's desk and has a look over her shoulder at her screen.

SAMANTHA
She's part of a very old case, unsolved murders
starting from the late seventies, stabbings. She was
the first victim by the looks of it. This is serious stuff
Matt, why would someone write her name on a
post-it note and stick it on my screen?

MATTHEW
I dunno mate, go and ask the DI before you get
your arse kicked for poking your nose in
without authorisation.

Samantha continues.

SAMANTHA
And what the hell is Operation Kestrel, the system
won't let me go any further, it says my access is
restricted, I've a bad feeling about this, Matt,
something is not right and I'm going to get to the
bottom of what this post-it note means. Freaked me
right out, she was my first victim? What the fuck.

EXT: UNIVERSITY CAMPUS - NIGHT - 1979

Outside of a sports hall on a University campus with a crowd of young people heading towards the entrance and queuing up to enter.

INT: SPORTS HALL - NIGHT - 1979

A large nosey crowd of young people standing in front of a stage at a punk rock concert with a band playing loud music. Camera zooms in on a group of three young girls enjoying themselves.

EXT: UNIVERSITY GROUNDS - NIGHT

Two girls, Sally Cameron and Fiona Harvey are walking along arm-in-arm and the third girl, Nancy Williams runs up after them and catches them up, they are all buzzing following the concert.

NANCY WILLIAMS
Hey Fiona, Sally wait up. That was bloody great, we are most definitely doing this again, shame we couldn't get any booze, but what a brilliant night.
To the three musketeers.

SALLY CAMERON
Isn't that the truth, three's perfect and four musketeers is most definitely a crowd.

NANCY

You are bad Sally, but right of course Annie can
be well, weird I suppose even if you ignore her
God-fearing mother and mouse-like Dad.

The three girls carry on walking chatting and laughing, they come to a road junction and stop walking.

SALLY

Nancy you want to come to ours and
stay over with us tonight?

NANCY

Nah sorry girls this is me, I'm done and need to get
home, I'm knackered; I'll see both
you lovelies tomorrow

Girls, hug, split up and Nancy goes one way and the two other girls go in different direction.

Nancy Williams is walking down a footpath at night with hedges on both sides, someone approaches from a distance at speed, running, right up to her, as she turns, and looks shocked she is stabbed with a large knife in the stomach. The perpetrator is unseen. She falls to the ground; the knife can be seen stabbing the girl further and then the person turns moving quickly in the direction they came from.

INT: LARGE OPEN SPACE CITY POLICE OFFICE - PRESENT - DAY

Detective Inspector Walcott walks through the office towards Samantha Blaketon.

SAMANTHA
Oh, Morning Ma'am, have you got a sec,
can I ask you something?

DI WALCOTT
Sure, DC Blaketon, what's up?

SAMANTHA
Not sure where to start and this is going to sound
really weird right, but bear with me, when I came
in today there was a post-it note on my PC, not
normally a biggy, but this asked me to look into
someone called Nancy Williams who was a
victim and was really important. Did you
leave it on my screen Ma'am?

DI WALCOTT
OK sounds weird, but not guilty I'm afraid I've not
heard of her... so did you look, who is she,
is she one of our cases or victims?

SAMANTHA
Well Guv, here's the thing I did find her, but not

in the minor crime/anti-social behaviour database. Because the note said she was their first victim, which freaked me out a bit as it was written as if from the perp, anyway I did a really naughty thing. I looked in the Police National Database without authorisation.

DI WALCOTT
Right stop there lady, you know that you are out of order on this don't you and searching the Police National Database without authority is a disciplinary offence let alone way above your remit and rank, do you want to get us all in front of Professional Standards?

SAMANTHA
I know Guv, I'm really sorry but please bear with me, I think this is really important, who on earth wrote the post it note and why my PC. It gets worse Ma'am sorry she is in the Major Crime database as a very old case and part of some classified Op called Kestrel and…

DI WALCOTT
Oh great, a Major Crime, bloody operation, for Christ's sake Sam you know how up their own arses they are, you done anything else to screw up my life this morning?

SAMANTHA
So, sorry Guv, but honestly why would someone in here leave a post-it note on my PC telling me to check a girl called Nancy Williams out and that she was the first victim it doesn't make any sense? It's also unsolved and part of a classified Operation... I don't have the authority to access all that secret squirrel major crime stuff, but you do?

DI WALCOTT
Sam, so not going to happen, listen it's going to stay a major crime case I don't want you poking about in the national database any further, and I don't want to hear the words Kestrel coming out of your mouth again are we clear. Are we clear Sam?

SAMANTHA
Yes, ma'am were clear.

DI WALCOTT
I have no idea who put the post-it note on your bloody computer, but this ends right here, right now, I am not winding up Major Crime, not today. And that is an order Sam.

EEXT: RESIDENTIAL CUL-DE-SAC - 1980 - DAY

Middle class residential Cul-de-sac, South East of England, semi-rural location.

INT: FRONT LIVING ROOM - 1980 - DAY

Living room scene with Fiona Harvey ironing, she has a Walkman on and is singing to herself. A television is on in the background (News headlines about Ronald Reagan becoming US President).

EXT: FRONT DOOR - 1980 - DAY

At the front door someone not seen is ringing the bell and knocking the door, they move to stand outside of the living room window. You can see the girl inside dancing and ironing, she looks up out of the window and smiles and waves, gesturing to come inside around the back.

The person moves walking around to the side of the house and in through the back door.

INT: FRONT LIVING ROOM - 1980 - DAY

Fiona Harvey is dancing, singing to herself while ironing, she removes her headphones.

FIONA
Come through don't be shy silly, I don't bite.

Person comes through into the living room and faces the girl who smiles at first and then her face turns to one of horror and shock, a large kitchen knife can be seen, Fiona is then stabbed many times in the stomach, the character with the knife is not seen.

A view of a blood-soaked Fiona Harvey lying on the front room floor.

EXT: RESIDENTIAL HOME - PRESENT - DAY

Home residential address of Samantha Blaketon, her car is seen driving up onto the drive and Samantha gets out. She walks up to the front door, un-locks it and enters inside, on the hallway table is a white piece of paper, she puts her keys down next to the note. You can see what is written on the note.

INT: NOTE SHOT

My second victim was much more enjoyable; Fiona Harvey was such a bitch.

EXT: RUN DOWN RESIDENTIAL HOUSING ESTATE - PRESENT - DAY

Samantha Blaketon and Matthew Ash are walking towards a group of youths at the rear of housing association homes in a parking area for residents. Sam catches up with Matt.

SAMANTHA
Matt, wait… listen I have got to talk to you about that note I got at work, really it's seriously worrying me, I got another note at home put through my door. I just don't know what to do Matt, why is this happening to me?

MATTHEW
Blimey, this is starting to sound really bad Sam must be serious, you never ask me for advice, look don't

worry let's deal with this lot and then go grab
a coffee and I'll be all ears.

SAMANTHA
Oh, very sensible Mr Big Ears…
OK thanks Matt, I appreciate it.

MATTHEW
You know what they say about men with big ears.

SAMANTHA
Whatever lover boy.

MATTHEW
Right you lot stay still, police, we need a word with
you all about the late night ASB and drinking
that is happening around here.
Let's start with some introductions
shall we… names and addresses, please?

Various un-complementary comments from the youths who begin to talk to Samantha and Matthew who are writing things down in their pocketbooks.

INT: COFFEE SHOP – PRESENT – DAY

Modern coffee shop busy with customers ordering at the counter, but also sitting at tables. Samantha Blaketon and Matthew Ash sitting at a table at the rear of the coffee shop.

SAMANTHA
This was pushed through my door the other night. To be honest it totally freaked me out, what the hell is going on here and who is bloody doing this, first at work and now at my home… what should I do Matt?

MATTHEW
Fuck, you need to talk to the DI about this shit, right now you need to cover your arse girl… I have a really bad feeling about all this shit. Someone is either winding you up or if real you could be in danger Sam, so let's get out of here and back to the office so you can talk to the DI.

SAMANTHA
Hang on a minute Matt I was thinking… I might just look up the files in the database to see if Fiona Harvey was also a murder victim?

MATTHEW
What the Fu… mate you know what the DI told you, do you not like working in our team anymore (pointing to a sign that says waitress wanted) dig into the files and you will be working here as my coffee bitch, now let's go.

They both walk out of the coffee shop and as they are passing an alleyway Sam pulls Matt into the alley and kisses him.

MATTHEW
Bloody hell Sam.

SAMANTHA
I love it when you are so macho Matt, look sorry my heads all over the place, just, so been wanting to do that for so long, I know I shouldn't have sorry.

MATTHEW
It's OK Sam I quiet enjoyed it actually.

(tries to pull Sam towards him)

SAMANTHA
No wait this is not right if my mum could see me now, she would say something like the man who commits adultery is an utter fool, for he destroys himself. Quote from Proverbs come on Mr big ears.

Sam walks off and Matt stands there with his arms outstretched totally confused and shocked.

EXT: POLICE TRAINING SCHOOL - 1981 - DAY

New uniformed young police cadets are on a parade ground with a Police sergeant instructor shouting marching orders to them trying to teach them to march.

SERGEANT
Attention, quick march, right turn…

The group of cadets come to attention and then start marching out of step.

INT: POLICE QUARTERS - 1981 - DAY

Two female police cadets are in shared quarters with two single beds and starting to change out of their police uniforms and into civilian clothes.

>JANE WOODWARD
>That was bloody hard, I just kept losing my steps and I don't know what on earth was going on with my bloody arms, they were like windmills, so embarrassing.

>FEMALE CADET 2
>I hate this part of the training, how is this going to help us join the regular police force, you don't see many cops marching down the high street on a Saturday night when the disco's chuck out do you.

>JANE
>Right's that's me all dolled up I'll see you later my lovely I'm off to meet Graham down the local, let's see if he's got any personality to go with those looks.

>FEMALE CADET 2
>Lucky girl ok see you later Jane…
>enjoy, but don't be late back.

EXT: TOWN CENTRE STREET - 1981 - EARLY EVENING

Jane Woodward is seen walking towards a pub on a high street with shops, restaurants and the pub. It is not busy and just turning dark. As she approaches the pub someone comes from behind at speed, running and she is pushed at force down a side alley, near the pub. You then see an unseen person with a large knife stabbing her repeatedly in the stomach.

INT: LARGE OPEN SPACE CITY POLICE OFFICE - PRESENT - DAY

Back to the police office - People sitting at desks in front of computers, usual busy office scene, telephones ringing, people moving about the office, uniformed officers walking through etc.

Samantha Blaketon is sitting in DI Walcott's office in front of her desk crying, DI Walcott is sitting behind her desk.

DI WALCOTT
Listen to me Sam, calm down, I don't really understand what you are saying start at the beginning, and tell me what's happened?

SAMANTHA
Gov I don't know what to do, it just doesn't make any sense to me? I was there I bloody knew this girl.

DI WALCOTT
Calm down Sam, I know it's difficult but you need to
explain what has happened so I can help you,
I don't understand what is up?

SAMANTHA
Sorry Gov, I got an email just now from…
well me, although it looks like it's from me,
but it's not, honest Gov.

DI WALCOTT
Sam you are not making any sense I hope it's nothing
to do with you accessing systems you don't have
permission for. If you got an email from yourself
then it's probably some sort of scam,
we could get IT to look at it.

SAMANTHA
No Gov, someone using my name which really
freaked me out… said Jane Woodward was his third
victim and that she was a stuck-up cow
who deserved what she got.

DI WALCOTT
OK so you think this is connected to the same
case mentioned in your post-it note, we better get
Forensics to look at the email, don't worry.

SAMANTHA
This is all crazy… An email to me from me about Jane, post-it note telling me to look at Nancy Williams, and I've not mentioned it, but I got a note stuck through my door at home saying that Fiona Harvey was victim number two and was a bitch and now this message about Jane, I was there Guv I knew her, this is freaking me out?

DI WALCOTT
Sam, sorry I need to get this straight in my head, we spoke about the post-it note, someone winding you up and I told you to drop it. Fiona Harvey never heard of her, when did you get this?

SAMANTHA
Sorry Gov I was going to come and see you and I know you are going to get annoyed, but I looked at the National Police Database again and Fiona Harvey is another unsolved murder case on Major Crime, now this email as I said I was bloody there Guv, Jane Woodward was a police cadet with me at training school in the early 1980s, she got murdered while off duty at a local pub and I don't need to look that up I know it's another unsolved murder and I know it's what our local nick at the time called the Kitchen Knife killer if I believe this sodding email Jane was victim number three.

DI WALCOTT
I will deal with you accessing the system again later now show me the email. Let me get this clear the post-it note told you about a Nancy Williams, the note through your door talked about Fiona Harvey and now this email has Jane's murder in it. As you have already looked at the major crime case and made the link these messages are clearly important so here's what we do. I will talk to the new DCI see what Major Crime have to say about all of this. Now listen to me Sam do not talk to anyone about this, understand, as the post-it note was placed by someone with access to these offices, we need to tread very carefully, let's see if we can get the email traced as a starter.

SAMANTHA
Thanks, Gov, oh sorry I told Matt Ash about the post-it note and the note put through my door, but not seen him since I got the email so he doesn't know about the that.

DI WALCOTT
Well don't tell him about the email and tell him to keep his mouth shut about the other two notes, I don't want this getting out until I have talked to the Major Crime DCI got it, good lets grab a cuppa and get that email looked at by IT.

INT: MAJOR CRIME OFFICE - PRESENT - DAY

Busy police office, with detectives sitting outside a separate office, inside the office DCI Campbell is sitting at his desk drinking coffee, with DI Walcott sitting in front of his desk.

DCI CAMPBELL
Sorry Inspector, let me get this straight one of your Detective Constables in the Anti-social behaviour team is seemingly receiving notes, which could be a wind up from well shall we say someone unknown hilarious cop… And these notes are about a Major Crime team unsolved old case, that could be linked to Operation Kestrel, I can tell you Inspector this is not funny.

DI WALCOTT
I don't think this is a wind up Gov, which is why I wanted to talk to you, Op Kestrel what is it?

DCI CAMPBELL
OK let's forget about a potential wind up Kestrel is a classified operation that we are running around a large number of unsolved murders where all the victims were stabbed repeatedly in the stomach with a large bladed kitchen knife… it all started in 1979. However, as the last one was committed fairly recently it's very much a live and ongoing case. We think the killer is the same person, but over the last 40 years numerous investigation teams have got

absolutely nowhere, so you will see Inspector why I don't find all this very funny. This could be a serious breach if a cop is behind it.

DI WALCOTT
Oh, Sorry Gov the kitchen knife killer case, never been involved, but obviously fairly infamous case around here. I never realised but are you saying there is no forensics, no DNA, no witnesses, surely that can't be right Gov?

DCI CAMPBELL
Nada, zip absolutely bloody nothing and Op Kestrel is strictly confidential so not a word outside this room, and a conversation for another day on how your officer even knows about it. As you may know these all seem like random stabbings and are spread across a 40-year period, but the MO is exactly the same. Lone female victim, alone in an isolated location, surprised we think and stabbed in the stomach repeatedly. No CCTV, No witnesses bloody nothing.

DI WALCOTT
Christ so what do you make of what Blaketon is saying, are you going to take it seriously about the contact potentially coming from the killer or do you think it's just a data breach, maybe from someone she knows in your team?

DCI CAMPBELL
Not sure, but those details are the three first victims, no one else outside of the operation would know, let alone link them together. My gut says this is not a serious breach to wind someone up. Major Crime will have to investigate, and I will get my best people to talk to your Constable Blaketon, pronto. This is why I have been bought in to head up Op Kestrel. What do you make of Blaketon can she be trusted?

DI WALCOTT
She's a good officer sir, I would back her one hundred percent and she is destined for much better things than my area of work, maybe even you're A team. Do you think she's been targeted because she was present at the Jane Woodward murder?

DCI CAMPBELL
Who the hell knows, but I don't believe in coincidences, so from this point forward we investigate and keep this just between us Inspector, is that understood? The investigation has virtually no new leads so this could be just what we need.

INT: TELESALES OFFICE - PAST 1986 - LATE AFTERNOON

A busy telesales office with banks of staff on the phone selling all talking and taking orders. A female employee, Hilary Todd gets up from her desk, waves goodbye to colleagues and leaves the sales office.

EXT: REAR OF THE SALES OFFICE BUILDING - PAST 1986 - NIGHT

Hillary Todd walks to her car in the dark, with her keys in her hand. A person follows her at a distance to begin with and then gets closer, quicker and quicker until the lone female turns in surprise and is stabbed repeatedly in the stomach.

INT: COUNCIL HOUSE - PAST - EARLY 1970s - EVENING

A young girl around 10 years old is sitting at a kitchen table eating her supper, with her mother standing at the sink washing up with her back to the girl.

MOTHER
You eating your supper, Princess?

GIRL
Yes Mum, but I don't really like the beans.

MOTHER (Without moving)
Listen you little bitch if you don't eat all of your supper you will remain the useless little shit you have always been.

Girl looks horrified and begins to cry, mother doesn't move from the sink.

MOTHER
Flee the evil desires of youth and pursue righteousness (making the sign of the cross on her chest) Timothy 2:22, now stop snivelling before I give you a good reason to cry for real

Girl tries to stop crying and continues to eat her supper.

MOTHER
There's my good girl eat your beans; they will make you very brainy you know. My mummy used to make me eat my tea to make me happy and healthy, love you darling.

Girl tries to smile and eat her beans.

MOTHER (Still at the sink)
Say it.

GIRL
Love you too Mum.

MOTHER
Good girl.

INT: TELESALES OFFICE - PAST 1986 - DAY

Same telesales office as before. Desks filled with people with headsets on in teams answering and talking on the telephone. A pretty woman, Ann Jones aged around 20 is sitting at a desk, wearing a headset talking on the telephone.

ANN JONES
Yes, I understand that you need the delivery, but as I have said our lorry has broken down and we will not be able to get your order to you until tomorrow I am really sorry.

Girl is nodding and pulling a face to a colleague opposite using her fingers to talk like a puppet mouthing blah… blah… blah.

ANN JONES
Yes, I do see and as I said we are sorry, look there is no need to swear at me… I will disconnect the call if you keep swearing at me. Charming she's hung up on me, don't you just hate women buyers, give me a man any day.

They both laugh, a different colleague, Sarah Brazier approaches their desks.

SARAH
How you both doing? I tell you I keep crapping myself every time I arrive in the morning and leave at night, I've even stopped going out for lunch. It

was so shocking what happened to poor Hilary Todd, being stabbed like that, have the police talked to you either of you yet?

ANN JONES
No, not me I wasn't even in work the day it happened, so they won't get much from me, anyway I didn't even like the women she was a bitch of a supervisor who clearly upset someone.

SARAH
You are so bad Ann.

EXT: RESIDENTIAL HOME - PRESENT - DAY

Home residential address of Samantha Blaketon, she drives onto her driveway and parks and gets out of the car. There is a person across the street in shrubbery looking towards Samantha. She is being watched. As she approaches her front door, there is a sound in the street, Sam turns and looks towards the bushes.

SAMANTHA
Hello is someone there? Hello, I'm a Police Officer I'm calling this in so show yourself before my colleagues get here and you get yourself into trouble.

Nothing happens, but the person stays hidden and keeps looking towards her. Sam turns and hurries to her front door, unlocking it and going inside, she turns on inside lights, the person then starts to move away from the house. Sam is looking concerned out of her window.

INT: MAJOR CRIME OFFICE - PRESENT - DAY

Modern open plan office full of plain clothed police officers in business suits. Glass side offices housing more senior officers. Secure office with signs saying authorised officers only in this area and offender photos and case boards showing wanted suspects on walls.

Meeting room with a large table with officers sitting around, DCI Campbell is at the front of the meeting talking through some slides of Operation Kestrel.

DCI CAMPBELL

So as some of you are new like me to Op Kestrel, I will give a brief summary of what we know and where we are right now. First murder was in 1979 Nancy Williams a young eighteen-year-old female who was out with her mates at a local concert, left her friends and was stabbed to death with what we believe was a large kitchen knife. No witnesses, no CCTV back in the day and no forensics. The investigation revealed, well not much really no obvious leads, enemies or suspects a random it would appear killing.

PC MACDONALD

Gov have we still got all of the evidence from the

original investigation, is it worth another look?

DCI CAMPBELL
Trust me don't waste your time, each individual piece of evidence has been forensically looked at by numerous teams over the years, the result, an absolute big fat zero.
let's get through this… victim two Fiona Harvey, a young women killed in 1980 a year after the first again with a large kitchen knife in her own home while ironing, same MO, victim three Jane Woodward a training police cadet killed in 1981, again a year after the last, she was off duty on her way to the pub to meet her boyfriend, large kitchen knife to the stomach, victim four Hilary Todd another young women killed in 1986, which was a change to the pattern… a five year gap, she was leaving work at a tele-sales company… yes you have guessed it stabbed in the stomach with a large kitchen knife.

WPC ABRAHAM
Gov, so all with the same MO large kitchen knife to the stomach, no evidence, but was there any links between the victims?

DCI CAMPBELL
The first two yes, they were school friends, but nothing could be established with the rest, all of the women appear to have absolutely no connection with

each other. Sorry to push on, but there is a lot to get through so hold your burning questions to the end as I have said all of this has been reviewed again and again previously. Forget about looking at boyfriends, family etc. all done ad nauseam. We need to focus on new leads. Moving on the 1990s saw another four killings, all women, all with the same MO various common kitchen knives, which are hard to trace of course, all committed in random places and with seemingly no connection and no clue as to who is committing these murders. Trust me this case has ended many a career, but I'm determined as I'm sure you are that this will not happen to us.

INT: COUNCIL HOUSE LIVING ROOM - PAST 1972 - EARLY EVENING

A young girl is sitting in the living room watching a black and white television with a children's programme playing. All is calm and then an argument and raised voices can be heard from the kitchen, which is just off the living room. A man and women are loudly arguing, then it goes quiet. The young girl goes from the living room to the kitchen door to look. She is not seen by the adults.

INT: COUNCIL HOUSE KITCHEN - PAST 1972 - EARLY EVENING

A small sized man has his back to the sink and a woman is standing in front of him threatening him with a large kitchen knife.

The women is extremely aggressive and manic, and the man looks very scared.

MOTHER
You fucking give me attitude again and
I will cut your guts like a sliced loaf.

FATHER
OK honey I'm so sorry, please… please put the knife
down, our Princess is next door, I'm so sorry
please darling don't hurt me again.

MOTHER
If we confess our sins, he is faithful
and just and will forgive us.

The girl looks horrified and silently edges back into the living room with her back against the wall, tears running down her face. All goes quite in the kitchen and eventually the girl is brave enough to look back into the kitchen.

INT: COUNCIL HOUSE KITCHEN - PAST 1972 - EARLY EVENING

The mother is standing at the sink washing up and is happily singing quietly to herself. The father is sitting at the kitchen table, un-harmed and eating his tea in silence. The mother turns to see the girl and the father looks up and smiles.

MOTHER
Hello, my Princess, you want anything to eat,
no then go back in doors and watch your
programme and let your Dad eat his supper.

The girl says nothing and looks between her Mother & Father.

FATHER
It's OK my Princess go and watch the telly, I'll come
through in a minute and watch with you.

INT: MAJOR CRIME OFFICE - PRESENT - DAY

Back to the meeting room and the briefing with officers about Operation Kestrel, officers talking amongst themselves some standing drinking coffee.

DCI CAMPBELL
OK all let's get back to it shall we as we still have a lot
to get through. Now the pattern we thought we had of
three murders each year and then a five-year gap was
sent into free fall between 2000 and 2010 as there was
absolutely nothing. Ten fucking years of nothing...
and before you ask they examined exhaustively
whether the killer might have been in prison, abroad,
sectioned you name it the previous teams have looked
at it,
again no clues, we have no bloody idea.
2011 the pattern starts again with the next victim Rosie

Denfield a forty five-year-old professional and I use that term lightly, a petty criminal more at home to causing a nuisance or shoplifting. She's also a drug user and part time prostitute. Well known to the police, a druggy who would nick an old grannies last pound to score.

DCI Campbell changes the slide on the presentation and the camera sees a page with three women's faces on it… Rosie Denfield, Susan Carpenter and Anna Schneider.

DCI CAMPBELL

2012 a year later, again sees the next victim, Susan Carpenter a fifty seven year old local Magistrate and trust me this ended the career of the previous DI and DCI. Again, no connections, nothing. 2013 and the next was Anna Schneider a nineteen year old German University student, studying believe it or not forensic science, bloody good what that lot did for her, again random killing, all three with large kitchen knives. No bloody evidence recovered on any of them. I'm sure you're all getting what the major problem is with this case.

WPC ABRAHAM

Gov, what I don't get is why didn't the media get a hold of all this at the time and through the years, all women all stabbed to death with a kitchen knife its tabloid heaven.

DCI CAMPBELL
And if I could have had my way, they would still be the case. We now have formally a serial killer dubbed the Kitchen Knife killer. Whoever is doing this, and I believe it was them, has just written and told the national press about all that has happened and how the police are so incompetent and couldn't catch a cold in a flu epidemic. They sent a handwritten note to one of the bloody daily national papers, with a kitchen knife that had Anna Schneider's blood on it, but nothing else. The note chronicled all of the killings since 1979. The bloody press have gone mad, and part of the reason we are all looking at this poisoned chalice case yet again.

INT: LARGE OPEN SPACE CITY POLICE - PRESENT - DAY

Back to the police office. Samantha is sitting at her desk on the computer, colleagues milling around. Matthew is sitting opposite working. Samantha's phone rings.

SAMANTHA
Hello, DC Blaketon how can I help you… hello can I help you, is there anybody there… I can hear you breathing look if you can't talk to me, I can't help you.

MOTHER
You're a she-devil, listen to me, Princess,

you're so dangerous, and God will have
his revenge on you, trust my words.

SAMANTHA
What the hell… hello, hello they've bloody
hung-up on me.

MATTHEW
Who has? you all right.

SAMANTHA
Err yes, yes, I'm fine.

MATTHEW
Well you don't look like it what was that all about…
bad news?

SAMANTHA
They called me a She-Devil and that I was in danger.

MATTHEW
What… someone who knows you well then. Look
sorry it's probably just some deranged person making
their daily nuisance call, you know we get a lot of
those, or somebody is winding you up.

SAMANTHA
Matt, I haven't said anything to you before, but I'm
convinced I'm being watched, even followed. I'm sure

someone has been watching my house.

MATTHEW

Blimey, you sure... I think you are just jumpy at the moment with all that's going on with those notes, don't let some looney toon get to you.

SAMANTHA

I have a bad feeling about this Matt I think I'm being targeted by the killer, just don't understand what's happening... why me?

MATTHEW

Go talk to DI Walcott, she will help you, if you think it is that serious. I can't see why the killer would contact you Sam, why now he's given nothing away all these years according to the media. Or I could come around to your house to protect you, but that will cost you wine, pasta and who knows what else.

SAMANTHA

Behave Romeo, just got this awful feeling... I'm convinced that I just spoke to the killer Matt and I don't bloody want to be his next victim.

INT: MAJOR CRIME OFFICE - PRESENT - DAY

Back to the meeting room and the briefing with officers about Operation Kestrel.

DCI CAMPBELL

So our last victim and with the highest profile, which I'm sure you are all aware of was Josie Abebe, killed just a few months ago. Ms Abebe was our elected local policing and crime commissioner and within these four walls is the main reason why so many resources have been made available to re-vamp this operation. I don't need to remind you all that despite our best efforts we still have very little. DS Reed is now going to take you through what little we have on the last victim.

DS Reed is a tall, well-built officer with Caribbean heritage. He stands from the table and comes to the front to join DCI Campbell.

DS REED

Thanks boss, so guys, let's focus on the last victim for a moment and why? Why Josie Abebe was it personal or was it because of the profile of her role? Why did the killer pick her, and you can use that question for all of our victims?

INT: BLAKETON'S DESK - PRESENT - DAY

Samantha is sitting at her desk typing on the computer when she stops typing as another email message pops on her screen looking like it has come from Samantha Blaketon. She looks shocked.

                    SAMANTHA
        Oh No not again… Gov you need to see this?

Matthew Ash, another colleague and DI Walcott come over to her screen to look at the message. The message is still visible on her screen its shows it's from DC Samantha Blaketon and is titled Next Victim.

                    DI WALCOTT
            Right, open it let's see what it says,
            then we can get forensics to look at it.

Samantha Blaketon opens the email and the contents says:

Computer screen YOU ARE NEXT TO DIE BITCH

                    DI WALCOTT
        Listen up everyone, from now I want DC Blaketon
        to be all of your new best friend, she goes nowhere
        on her own… all visits and work to be doubled
        crewed. Sam uniform will be keeping an eye on
        your home address. No arguments, we take no
        chances and we take this threat to one of our own
        very seriously. I do not need to tell you how many
        murders this killer is responsible for… right let's
        tighten everything down and take no chances…
                 and that goes for everyone.

EXT: WOODLAND - RECENT PAST - DAY

Large woodland and countryside setting with dog walkers and mountain bikers enjoying the space.

Josie Abebe a 30 something black woman is seen in outdoor casual clothes walking along a path with her dog. A couple of mountain bikers pass her, and she carries on walking. She is approached by June Kennedy, an older female dog walker who knows her.

JUNE KENNEDY
Hi Josie, good to see you're getting some time away to spend with Keith. Who's a good boy then Keithy.

JOSIE ABEBE
Hello June, lovely to see you and Willow, yes, I have to grab what little time I get to myself these days.

JUNE KENNEDY
I'm sure the police know what to do when you are not there dear, anyway have a good walk with Keith see you.

JOSIE ABEBE
Bye June, take care see you soon.

Josie continues in the other direction with her walk.

A mountain biker is seen from the back heading towards Josie, she makes Josie jump as she gets near her and jumps off the bike and rushing up to Josie. The biker stabs her in the stomach a few times with a large bladed knife.

Later on, another dog walker sees Josie on the ground and bends down to help her.

>   JOSIE ABEBE
>   I know who...

>   SECOND DOG WALKER
>   Don't try and talk the police and
>   paramedics are coming.

>   JOSIE ABEBE
>   Bla... blay...

INT: MAJOR CRIME OFFICE - PRESENT - DAY

Back to the meeting room and the briefing with officers being given by DS Reed.

>   DS REED
>   We know that the Police & Crime Commissioner
>   Josie Abebe was clearly well liked by the public
>   despite her sweeping proposals to cut policing
>   numbers and to reduce non-essential police teams.
>   Her killing was a massive shock for everyone and
>   again despite all of the people using Lewis Woods no
>   one saw the incident and all of the descriptions of
>   bikers and dog walkers given, well by bikers and dog
>   walkers that came forward were useless. As with all of

the previous MOs used by the killer, no forensics, no witnesses... nothing as usual.

However, the dog walker that found Josie said something like I know who, and she thinks she was trying to say something like blame before she died. Blame who, herself, someone else who knows, no further lines of enquiry could be matched to those comments, so again we appear to have very little.

INT: DI WALCOTT'S POLICE OFFICE – PRESENT – DAY

DI Walcott is sitting behind her desk with DC Blaketon sitting opposite. A male Asian officer, DS Attri is sitting next to DC Blaketon.

DI WALCOTT
Sam this is DS Attri he is with Professional Standards.

DS ATTRI
DC Blaketon you are not under caution or do not need your Federation rep with you, this is... shall we say an informal chat given the unprecedented circumstances we find ourselves in. You appreciate why I am here yes? Our audit shows unauthorised access to the Police National Database on numerous occasions... by you.

SAMANTHA
You don't understand what is happening to me, I'm being targeted or I'm some sort of key to the knife killer case, they have chosen me with notes on the victims, I'm being followed I'm sure… I know I am going to be next I have to…

DI WALCOTT
Sam, we understand what you are going through and how upset you must be, but we agreed that you would not search the database again after you told me you had searched for the initial victims, this unauthorised access has to stop?

DS ATTRI
Sorry Ma'am but its far more serious than a couple of unauthorised searches, as I said numerous searches have taken place by DC Blaketon, without the correct authorisation, she has also tried and failed on numerous times to access a classified Operation's files… I may have no option but to recommend a formal investigation and suspension.

SAMANTHA
Look I'm sorry, but you're not getting the serious situation I'm in, I don't understand why but I'm sure that I'm the key to all this and I need to access the information, I know if I could see everything I can help and solve this case.

DI WALCOTT

OK Sam calm down, DS Attri I wasn't aware of the multiple searches please give me some time before you make your recommendations, let me talk to DCI Campbell, I think I have an idea that will resolve this difficult situation that we will all be happy with?

INT: MAJOR CRIME OFFICE - PRESENT - DAY

In the meeting room DCI Campbell who gets up and takes over the briefing from DS Reed.

DCI CAMPBELL

Thanks, Reedy, right one last thing over the last week or so we have had some new developments. We think the killer has started to target one of our DCs in the community safety unit. DC Samantha Blaketon, anyone know her… no matter, she has received two notes and a yet unidentified email telling her to look into the first victims. We also think she is being followed and received a weird phone call who she is convinced was from the killer.

Blaketon said a male, probably with mental health issues and full of talk about the devil… just what we need, anyway following a chat with her DI and a recent threat to Blaketon via email stating she's the next victim. I have agreed that Blaketon will be joining the Major Crime Team from tomorrow as I

want her close to our investigation, as I said she is
bright, but needs keeping a close eye on and most
importantly for the investigation her boss thinks
she can help us. I shouldn't have to remind you
all that we still have nothing so right now
we need all the help we can get.

EXT: POLICE STATION STAFF CAR PARK - PRESENT - NIGHT

DCI Campbell is walking away from the police office towards his car when he bumps into a Phil Webber a Digital Forensic officer walking across the car park towards the office.

DCI CAMPBELL
Hi-ya Phil… another late one?

PHIL WEBBER
Hello sir, of course and always when I want
to get home and watch the footy.

DCI CAMPBELL
Typical, look I won't keep you, any luck with that
Blaketon email… could really do with an update?

PHIL WEBBER
No worries sir, from my initial look and I'm still
running some in depth system tests it looks very
sophisticated to me, never seen anything like it.

DCI CAMPBELL
Presume you are going to tell me that it's pinging off servers across the World and you can't trace it?

PHIL WEBBER
I could cope with that, no sir, it's using our server and our system and if you believe our audit software then DC Blaketon sent it to herself, which clearly she didn't, this is what makes it so sophisticated and hard to track. It is somehow mirroring our system, but I will crack it just need some more time.

DCI CAMPBELL
Could someone have hacked our system or got hold of DC Blaketon's username and password.

PHIL WEBBER
Unlikely sir, again who ever has done this has been very clever the system shows that only one entry login for DC Blaketon when the emails were sent, again making it look like she's sending them to herself, bloody clever.

DCI CAMPBELL
Ok Phil, thank you and sorry to hold you up, hope you get home for the second half.

DCI Campbell starts to walk towards his car and Phil Webber turns towards the office.

> PHIL WEBBER
> Fat chance.

INT: COUNCIL HOUSE GIRLS BEDROOM - PAST 1976 - EVENING

Pretty 14-year old girl sitting in her bedroom listening to Lowdown, by Boz Scaggs on the radio, while reading a book and laying on her bed. Her bedroom door opens, and her smiling mother enters carrying a pile of clean ironed clothes, neatly stacked.

> MOTHER
> Hello, my Princess.

The girl turns the radio off.

> GIRL
> I was just doing my reading homework Mum.

> MOTHER
> Were you, do I look like an idiot
> you silly little disgusting bitch?

Mother hurls the neatly stacked clothes at the girl and then stands over the girl.

> MOTHER
> And no wonder, for even Satan disguises
> himself as an angel of light.

The Mother walks away to the bedroom door.

> MOTHER
> Tea in ten minutes Princess.

EXT: POLICE OFFICE STAFF CAR PARK - PRESENT - DAY

Samantha Blaketon parks her car, gets out and walks towards the police office. Matthew Ash calls from across the car park. She stops and turns around to talk to him.

> MATTHEW
> Ooh hello it's the new girl, all grown up and playing with the big kids, are we?

> SAMANTHA
> Shut up you I'm really nervous, do I look OK?

> MATTHEW
> You look gorgeous darling; don't worry you'll be fine. Don't worry yourself I will do all of your work as usual; you fancy a drink later?

> SAMANTHA
> Owe you one Matty, maybe talk later see ya, wouldn't want to be ya.

INT: MAJOR CRIME OFFICE - PRESENT - DAY

DCI Campbell is in his office with a letter in a plastic folder, DS Reed walks in.

DCI CAMPBELL
Reedy we have just got this letter sent up from forensics it's addressed to Blaketon and arrived by post this morning, but was intercepted by the crime scene unit, no DNA or prints, there's a surprise, but the contents is interesting.

DS REED
Emmm yes interesting I suppose, but it's just more threats against her. She starts with us, today doesn't she? Do you think we should be doing more to protect her Gov?

DCI CAMPBELL
No, err, I'm just a bit confused, give me the letter, look is it me, but something is not right; listen to what it says.
The bitch Blaketon is a dead woman walking, protect her well.

DS REED
As I said Gov, just a threat that Blaketon is supposedly next?

DCI CAMPBELL
But how does the killer know that we are keeping Blaketon close and have put measures in place to protect her?

DS REED
Oh I see what you mean Gov that is odd, perhaps it's just part of his game about goading us about her being next and that the police can't protect her?

DCI CAMPBELL
Yes maybe perhaps I'm reading too much into it, but looking over and reviewing all of the case files we have absolutely nothing, no clues, leads, witnesses… nothing, why is the killer now giving us information and talking to us, it doesn't feel right Reedy?

DS REED
I see what you are saying Gov, it does seem odd. Do you think Blaketon has told too many people in the community safety unit and somehow the information about her transfer and protection has got out… but that's hard to believe?

DCI CAMPBELL
No, Reedy, you know what my gut is like, not that, seriously my gut is telling me bad things are about to happen, something just doesn't feel right.

> DS REED
> Like what?

> DCI CAMPBELL
> I think… and God I hope I am wrong, but our killer maybe one of us a serving police officer or someone very close to us like a civilian employee or maybe even an ex-cop.

EXT: STREET NEAR BLAKETON'S HOME - PRESENT - NIGHT

Blaketon pulls up in her car in a streetlamp lit road and parks the car, as she gets out someone is watching her from down the road seemingly between two parked cars. Blaketon looks around nervously and thinks she sees the person watching her.

> SAMANTHA
> I can see you I'm calling it in.

There is a figure in the shadows standing still and watching Blaketon start to walk away… and then starts to follow her. Blaketon is now walking fast, almost running towards her home looking scared and over her shoulder. The stalker follows.

> SAMANTHA
> It's DC Blaketon I need help someone is following me, I did what I was told and parked a street away from my house, but they're here, please help me.

Blaketon is still on the phone but gets to her house, she quickly opens her front door, and slams it shut, she turns all of the lights on and goes into the kitchen and picks up a large kitchen knife. She is still on the phone.

INT: BLAKETON'S HOME - PRESENT - NIGHT

SAMANTHA
I've made it inside, please send a unit to my home address now; they're outside my house... Yes, I understand just bloody send someone will you?

EXT: OUTSIDE BLAKETON'S HOME
- PRESENT- NIGHT

There is a dark figure across the road from Blaketon's house, watching. The figure approaches the front path and her front door, the figure is looking at the front door.

INT: BLAKETON'S HOME - PRESENT - NIGHT

Blaketon is in her hallway looking at the front door that has a large glass panel, holding the large kitchen knife in her hand. You can hear police sirens in the distance.

SAMANTHA
I know you are out there, my colleagues are coming, you don't stand a chance, you cannot get to me.

Samantha's mother presses her face and hands on the glass of the front door suddenly and looks very angry.

> MOTHER
> You always was a selfish needy little bitch; God will punish those who do not obey the Gospel of our Lord Jesus.

> SAMANTHA
> Mother?

EXT: INSIDE POLICE PATROL CAR WITH LIGHTS AND SIRENS - PRESENT - NIGHT MOVING

> UNIFORMED POLICE OFFICER
> Foxtrot Alpha four zero, ETA zero two minutes, over.

INT: COUNCIL HOUSE REAR GARDEN - PAST - 1977

A pretty 15-year-old girl is sitting in the rear garden playing with a tape cassette recorder, which is playing Do you wanna make love by Peter McCann. Her mother comes out carrying washing to hang out on the line. The girl lets the song play while looking defiantly at her mother. The mother starts to hang out the washing and facing away from the girl.

> MOTHER
> You play your Devil tunes Princess;

they have no effect on me.

GIRL
I don't care what you think.

The Mother turns looking deranged and very angry and rushes towards the girl and grabs her around the throat.

MOTHER
You slut of the devil, you think with your filthy songs and whore clothes you can take on me and God…
I will always be too strong for you my girl.

The mother lets go but starts to laugh crazily out loudly.

INT: BLAKETONS KITCHEN - PRESENT - NIGHT

Blaketon is panicking and falling back towards the floor and screaming, a large kitchen knife is in her side, blood is showing on her white top.

EXT: POLICE CAR - PRESENT - NIGHT

The police car pulls up fast to Blaketon's home with blue lights flashing and two uniformed police officers jump out of the car and run towards the house, the front door is open. There is no one to be seen.

INT: BLAKETON'S KITCHEN – PRESENT – NIGHT

Blaketon is seen holding the kitchen knife in her hand, blood is on her white top, she plunges the knife in her side for a second time.

SAMANTHA
The idiots, for they eat the bread of wickedness, I win again, and drink the wine of violence, the next victim is me; Mother would be so proud.

The uniformed police officers enter.

UNIFORMED POLICE OFFICER
Police this is the police; Tasers have been drawn.

One police officer comes in the kitchen and sees only Blaketon on the floor covered in blood. He holsters the Taser and kneels down to help Blaketon. He puts his radio to his mouth.

UNIFORMED POLICE OFFICER
Foxtrot Alpha four zero priority, urgent assistance required from Paramedics an officer is down with stab wounds.

RADIO OPERATOR
Received four zero EMS on route.

UNIFORMED POLICE OFFICER
Hold on Sam.

> SAMANTHA
> Did you get him?

The second uniformed police officers comes into the kitchen.

> 2ND UNIFORMED POLICE OFFICER
> House clear, couldn't find anyone, the dog unit has just checked the garden and surrounding area, but nothing found.

INT: INSIDE AMBULANCE - PRESENT - NIGHT

> PARAMEDIC
> Can you hear me Sam, you have lost a lot of blood, but I am controlling the bleeding, we will be at the hospital very soon?

> SAMANTHA
> He just attacked me; I couldn't stop him… did they get him.

> PARAMEDIC
> Sam, come on Sam don't worry about all that stay with me Sam.

INT: MAJOR CRIME OFFICE - PRESENT - DAY

DCI Campbell is standing at the front of officers in a briefing room, present are DS Reed and DI Walcott along with a mixture of uniformed and plain clothed officers.

DCI CAMPBELL

OK guys can I have everyone's attention, thank you for coming in at such short notice, right… so this is what we know. DC Blaketon was attacked two hours ago by an unknown male, we have no description as yet, but hoping to talk to Blaketon shortly. The male was waiting for her at a side street near to where she lives. So, loads of thoughts, how did the killer know that DC Blaketon had been advised to park away from her home address? I want us to go through everything again, the notes, emails, threats we are missing something here people, and I want this just kept to within this team, information appears to be seeping out of our investigation and it needs to stop, DS Reed.

DS REED

Thanks Gov… having looked at the last note me and the Gov feel that it just contains too much information. The MO from all of the other murders is that we get nothing, no clues, witnesses, nothing. Why now all of a sudden are we getting detail… Er also the Gov thinks that the killer knows too much about what is going on within our investigation, so could be a serving police officer or retired or a police civilian or maybe forensics or someone close to us.

DCI CAMPBELL
Only a theory at the moment, but we have nothing else unless anyone has any other ideas? No thought not so as I have just said please please please let's keep my little theory just in these four walls for now. Right also most of you know DI Walcott, given what's happened to Sam Blaketon, given that she knows Sam well as her DI and more importantly DI Walcott's background working in our Behavioural Science Unit previously I have asked her to be seconded to Major Crime for the duration.

DI WALCOTT
Er thanks for the build-up Gov, in the circumstances happy to be here is not right, but you know that I will do all I can to help catch this madman, Sam is one of ours, he could have targeted any one of us, so we need to focus on the evidence for once he has given us I am convinced this is his first and only mistake so far.

DS REED
On behalf of the team welcome Ma'am.

DCI CAMPBELL
OK enough of the corporate smooth welcome package, we have work to do, you all have your actions, let's go people, let's get over to the hospital and talk to Blaketon.

INT: HOSPITAL WARD - PRESENT - DAY

Samantha Blaketon is sitting up in bed with a nurse taking her blood pressure and looking after her. An armed uniformed officer is standing outside of her room on guard.

INT: HOSPITAL WARD NURSE STATION - PRESENT - DAY

DCI Campbell and DI Walcott enter the station and approach a Doctor who is standing at the station with other nurses. They show their police ID.

DCI CAMPBELL
Hi Doc I'm DCI Campbell and this is my colleague DI Walcott we are leading the team on the attack on one of our officers DC Blaketon.

DOCTOR
Hi, I am Dr Chen the Senior Emergency Medicine Consultant, here and I'm responsible for overseeing the care of your officer Blaketon, how can I help.

DI WALCOTT
Just need to know how Sam is and we really need to talk to her Doc, we are desperate for anything she can give us, how bad is she, we don't want to rush her, but this is really urgent?

> DOCTOR
> She is not bad at all, superficial wounds to her stomach and side, which we have stitched she will need a tetanus injection, but she should be able to go home later.

> DCI CAMPBELL
> Er OK well... good news, clearly a lucky woman, can we see her?

> DOCTOR
> Of course, no problem she is on the general ward through those doors.

HOSPITAL WARD - PRESENT - DAY

Samantha Blaketon is in bed and DCI Campbell & DI Walcott come in and approach her bed. Blaketon smiles on seeing them.

> DI WALCOTT
> Hi Sam, how you doing?

> SAMANTHA
> Hi boss, yes, I'm good, hello sir.

> DCI CAMPBELL
> Hello Sam, good to see you are doing well, very lucky from what we hear, appreciate you are probably sore and stressed about what happened, but we really need to talk to you about the attack.

SAMANTHA
My mother said to me once that peoples sins, and painless acts will be remembered no more.
He will pay for attacking me.

DCI Campbell and DI Walcott look at each other very confused.

SAMANTHA
Right I can give a full description, do you want to take some notes in your pocketbook?

DI WALCOTT
Um yes sorry Sam if you are sure you are up to it then go for it.

SAMANTHA
When I pulled up and got out of my car I knew someone was watching me, I could just feel it, I dashed toward my house when I saw a man in the distance just standing watching me... got to my front door while on the phone to control asking for a response team to be sent.
I heard the police unit coming, I had a kitchen knife in my hand... ironic I know, so when he came to my door I opened it to get a good look at him... problem was he was all dressed in black and had a full ski mask on.

DCI CAMPBELL
OK Sam slow down, was there anything about him

that you recognised or that sticks out in your mind.

SAMANTHA
No Gov I could see he was white about six foot tall, medium build but that was it, he had a full black get up like SWAT or something and black gloves... he grabbed me and got the knife off me and tried to stab me in the stomach, but I managed to fight back and turn sideways... the police unit was almost with us, the siren got loud, he panicked I think and ran for it. It was so terrible.

DI WALCOTT
It's OK Sam, calm down you are safe now and were very lucky by the sounds of it that's all for now, when you are home I will pop by to see you, if you think of anything important, let us know will you. You are the only witness who has seen the killer so it is vital you think through every detail, anything that could help the investigation.

SAMANTHA
Yes, will do boss thanks for coming sir.

Samantha Blaketon is now on her own and starts singing quietly while hugging herself and rocking she is singing Three Blind Mice.

SAMANTHA
I need to see you Mother, need to deal with you, can't let you get in the way, not now

it's getting interesting.

EXT: SHELTERED HOUSING SCHEME GARDEN - PRESENT - DAY

A pretty manicured garden with elderly people sitting and reading, walking around and enjoying the space. An elderly lady in her late seventies is sitting on her own at the end of a bench. Samantha Blaketon approaches the bench she is sitting on and sits away from the lady at the other end of the bench.

> SAMANTHA
> Hello Mother.

The lady turns in surprise, then smiles.

> MOTHER
> Hello, my Princess, good to see you again.

> SAMANTHA
> I thought that I made myself very clear at Dad's funeral that I never wanted to see you again, so you can imagine how disappointed I was to see you the other night, you've been watching my home and coming to my front door haven't you?

> MOTHER
> Oh, my little darling Princess, you know you will always be my girl but never forget anyone who does

not do what is right is not a child of God…
John 3:10.

> SAMANTHA
> Enough.

Samantha slowly rises from her seat and walks calmly up to behind where her mother is sitting, the Mother doesn't move but smiles. Samantha pulls a large kitchen knife from her bag and stabs her mother repeatedly in her back.

> SAMANTHA
> In your words mother I'm taking a life for a life, an eye for an eye, tooth for a tooth bitch.

INT: VILLAGE GREEN WITH A SMALL SHOP - PRESENT - DAY

DI Walcott and DS Reed are walking along the road by the village green and approach a woman, Donna Sampson who is in her mid-sixties. She is standing next to her daughter and a couple of grandchildren. DI Walcott shows her police ID.

> DI WALCOTT
> Mrs Donna Sampson, police?

> DONNA SAMPSON
> Oh my God what has happened?

DS REED
Don't worry Mrs Sampson nothing has happened all is well; we just want to talk to you about your sister Nancy Williams?

DONNA SAMPSON
Bloody hell you scared the life out of me, you know she has been passed for many years, don't you, has something happened with her case?

DAUGHTER
I'll take the kids to get an ice cream, Mum.

The daughter and the kids walk away.

DI WALCOTT
Sorry just to spring this on you, I know it has been a long time, but we are following up on some background on her case.

DONNA SAMPSON
Blimey you are about forty years too late for your investigation love.

DI WALCOTT
We appreciate it's a long time ago, but the case is still open, as you know no one has ever been caught for your sister's murder and a new Major Crime Task Force is now reviewing the case?

DONNA SAMPSON
You didn't answer my question has something
happening with her case. Oh my God
has the killer murdered again?

DI WALCOTT
No nothing like that we are just reviewing all of
the evidence again to make sure all lines of enquiry
where followed up, could you tell us about
your sister and her friends?

DONNA SAMPSON
Oh those girls were a handful you know, the local
boys didn't really stand a chance, but of course you
know that Fiona Harvey, lovely girl was murdered
a year later, what happened had a massive effect on
Sally Cameron who was one of the three girls out
that night… she thought bless her she was going
to be the next victim, must have really
affected her life, poor love.

DS REED
Yes, we are now aware of the link between the girls,
we will of course be speaking again to Sally, is
there anything you can think of about that night
or anyone else we should talk too who was
connected to the girls?

DONNA SAMPSON
umm no dear not that I can think of after all this time we all went over it a thousand times with the police at the time... just wrong place,
wrong time, I guess.

DI WALCOTT
OK Donna, thank you, sorry that we sprung this on you without warning it was a bit of a long shot, but obviously if you can think of anything else, let us know, please be assured we are not letting this go, we will investigate until we catch the person responsible hope we didn't upset you.

DONNA SAMPSON
Don't worry dear and thank you for keeping on trying, as I said to my daughter a while back a sad end to the four amigos as they were known. Sorry that is what everyone used to call the four of them.

DS REED
Four?

DONNA SAMPSON
Ann Jones was the fourth amigo, but she was ill or something that night and didn't go to the concert, thick as thieves those four at school, but I suppose Ann was always on the outside but as it goes a lucky forth amigo, nevertheless.

DI WALCOTT
Ann Jones? Do you know if she was interviewed at the time as I don't recall her name in the statements I have read about the incident?

DONNA SAMPSON
Not sure my love I would have thought so, we were all spoken to by the police over and over again. I haven't seen her in years, such a pretty girl, but a bit strange… poor cow never stood a chance… her mother… well let's just say she had mental health issues in between her bible bashing and her father was a victim of domestic violence, poor chap.

INT: MAJOR CRIME OFFICE - PRESENT - DAY

DI Walcott is talking to officers in the busy office when Samantha Blaketon walks in to work, DI Walcott is shocked to see her.

SAMANTHA
Morning Ma'am.

DI WALCOTT
Sam what the hell are you doing here?

SAMANTHA
Doc said I was OK to work, I'm fine honestly Gov, just a bit sore, but I'm OK… I'd rather be here, feel safer here and I just want to help?

DI WALCOTT
I understand Sam, but it is too soon to be back to work surely. But I understand your concern OK as long as you are all right then I suppose you can stay, desk duties only mind… but it is good to have you back and you are safe here I promise… and I'm always glad of the extra pair of hands on this one.

SAMANTHA
Thanks Gov… where is everyone, anything I can do to help?

DI WALCOTT
DS Reed and I have just got back from some follow up enquiries and we may have a new significant lead; which DS Reed is currently following up on?

SAMANTHA
Oh… that er that is good, what have you found out?

DI WALCOTT
Early days on it Sam, but it appears we might have missed an important witness that is connected to the first two murders, a fourth friend of the girls who again appears not to have come on the investigation radar at the time.

SAMANTHA
Really Err can I help, I mean help track this girl

down, do some of the leg work, well
from my computer anyway?

DI WALCOTT
Girl? I didn't say it was a girl, do you know
something Sam. Sam has the killer sent you anything
else, you must tell me, you won't get into
trouble, but I need to know.

SAMANTHA
Err oh no sorry Gov, nothing like that, just assumed
it was a girl as there was three girls out on a night
out... I read all of the files previously... when you
told me not to... sorry Gov, but I know this case
inside out... I can help trust me Gov.

DI WALCOTT
OK you are forgiven for now, but not sure
Professional Standards would agree. It is a girl
one of their friends called Jones, Ann Jones.

SAMANTHA
Oh, I know I can help with that Ma'am.

EXT: OUTSIDE OF AN INNER-CITY OFFICE BUILDING - PRESENT - DAY

DS Reed is walking up a busy street, his phone rings and he stops outside of an office building to answer it.

DS REED
DS Reed... Hi yes I've managed to track down a Robert Hancock he used to be the commercial manager of Willard & sons the telesales company Hillary Todd the fourth victim worked for... he now works in town for some financial company... I'm just on my way in to see him... yes will update you when I get back.

DS Reed continues to walk and enter the office building.

INT: SMALL GLASS OFFICE - PRESENT - DAY

Robert Hancock is sitting behind a desk when his secretary let's DS Reed into the office. He stands and holds out a hand to shake DS Reed's hand.

ROBERT HANCOCK
Hi Bob Hancock, please take a seat... coffee?

DS REED
No, I'm fine thanks.

ROBERT HANCOCK
Thanks Alison PC Reed is it; how can I help you?

DS REED
Detective Sergeant Reed I work for the Major Crime team, nothing to worry about Mr Hancock...

unless you have something to confess?

ROBERT HANCOCK
Err no sorry sergeant I don't think so.

DS REED
Relax Bob I just need to ask you some questions on an old case I'm doing some research on.

HANCOCK/REED (said together)
Hilary Todd.

DS REED
Err yes, sorry I appreciate these things stay with you and I know it was thirty-five years ago… but there has been some developments and we have decided to take another fresh look over everything.

ROBERT HANCOCK
Oh right, yes sorry a nasty business… you're right It often just pops back in my mind what happened to poor Hilary. So, what has happened, what are these developments has someone been caught?

DS REED
Sadly, not it's still an unsolved case, we are just reviewing some of the initial incidents to make sure nothing was missed. I can't seem to find an employee list from the time of your company, although

I am sure you provided one.

ROBERT HANCOCK

No not that I'm aware of, it would have come through me all I remember is you lot interviewing everyone who was at work that day, numerous times. Can't say I remember being asked for any lists or anything.

DS REED

OK that's unusual it's just standard practice to get an employee list, but not to worry now I'm here could you tell me what Hilary was like, was she popular or have any enemies that sort of thing?

ROBERT HANCOCK

Nice girl as I recall and a bloody good supervisor, not that the telesales agents would agree, she run a very tight ship and didn't take any crap from any of them, but no she had no enemies that I am aware of… it was a friendly family run company, we worked hard but we were very social and pretty much all got along. Your colleagues went over and over all this at the time.

DS REED

OK thank you Mr Hancock sorry for making you re-think about what happened all those years ago, and wasting your time, but if you can think of anyone who didn't get on with Hilary or remember anything that might be of use no matter how small please give me a call.

ROBERT HANCOCK
Yes of course I will no worries.

DS REED
Oh, nearly forgot… a long shot but does the name Ann Jones mean anything to you?

ROBERT HANCOCK
Ann yes of course how could anyone forget Ann Jones our best telesales agent by a country mile and I have to say very pleasing on the eye…
don't tell me she is a victim?

DS REED
No… no not a victim, we are trying to trace her, but to be clear she worked for you and knew Hilary back in 1986?

ROBERT HANCOCK
Yes, she was in Hilary's team as I remember it was Hilary or Ann for the supervisor's job. We went with Hilary as I didn't want to lose Ann from the phones as she was brilliant at it. Don't think Ann took it very well. But she didn't fall out with Hilary as far as I know.

EXT: OUTSIDE OF AN INNER-CITY OFFICE
BUILDING - PRESENT - DAY

DS Reed comes outside of the building hurrying, he places a call and puts his mobile to his ear.

INTERCUT TO: MAJOR CRIME OFFICE - PRESENT- DAY

DC Blaketon picks up a ringing phone.

SAMANTHA
DC Blaketon, Major Crime.

DS Reed is walking and talking on his phone.

DS REED
Sam it's Reedy, what the hell are you doing back? Look that doesn't matter now did DI Walcott fill you in about an Ann Jones who was a friend of Nancy Williams and Fiona Harvey, our first two victims.

SAMANTHA
Yes, Skip she mentioned that you were following things up, but I can't see how it will help us with the case now. Perhaps the poor girl she just wanted to keep her head down and stay out of it and…

DS REED
Sam listen I have just spoken to the ex-boss of Hilary Todd the fourth victim and Ann Jones worked for them and was in Hilary's team.

                    SAMANTHA
        OK bloody hell... er coincidence then maybe
                this is not such a big town.

                     DS REED
    Sam she's connected in all this somehow and I need
    you to start a deep search into Ann Jones we need
    to find out who she is and where she is, we need to
      talk urgently with this women, she is involved in
    the killings somehow I just know it. This is the first
     major lead we have had on this case in bloody years.

                    SAMANTHA
    Yes of course, leave it with me Skip, but I'm not sure
     what use she will be now it was a very long time ago
    and no one knows better than me that our killer is a
     man, I have the scares to prove it... yes will do I'm
           on it now, see you when you get back... bye

Blaketon gets up, screws up and the paper she was making notes on in the bin, walks over to put her coat on and goes out of the office.

EXT: LARGE REAR GARDEN - PRESENT - EARLY EVENING

The garden has flower beds and a nicely kept lawn that is connected to a large bungalow. A woman with grey hair and in her late sixties is tending to the flowers and doing some light gardening. Samantha is at the side of the bungalow and comes into the rear garden, she approaches the woman from behind and makes her jump.

SAMANTHA
Hello Ma'am.

KATIE GRAHAM
Ooh Jesus… you really made me jump,
do I know you, what do you want.

SAMANTHA
Sorry don't worry I'm police, you do not recognise
me Ma'am do you. I'm disappointed with me being
your best police cadet at training school.

KATIE GRAHAM
Do you know how many police cadet's and
constables I have trained over the years, you can't
expect me to remember them all… although there
is something about you that looks familiar, but as
I say this is my private home and I don't appreciate
un-announced visits even from the police young lady.

SAMANTHA
Always playing the hard bitch.

KATIE GRAHAM
Look I don't need this shit, in the job or
not think you better leave.

SAMANTHA
Jane Woodward she was your cadet of the year remember, that should have been me, but hey, didn't do her any good did it?

Samantha pulls out a large kitchen knife and goes towards Katie.

KATIE GRAHAM
Wait, listen to me you don't want to do this, who are you, let's talk, talk about Jane.

SAMANTHA
Samantha Ann Jones ring any bells Inspector, you know the cadet that killed Jane, don't you worry yourself I'm just tidying up some loose ends just in case you wanted to talk to Major crime when they come visiting.

Blaketon stabs the retired Inspector with the kitchen knife and kills her. Blaketon walks away whistling and smiling.

INT: MAJOR CRIME OFFICE - PRESENT - DAY

DS Reed and DI Walcott are in the DCI Campbell's office. DCI Campbell is behind his desk.

DCI CAMPBELL
So that's very interesting about Ann Jones well done the both of you, why wasn't this picked up or connected at the time do we think?

DS REED
Not sure Gov, back in the 70s and early 80s no real computerised systems that double checked all associations and links, it was all a bit manual. I think she may have just fallen through the slats.

DCI CAMPBELL
Where are we with the background checks on Ann Jones?

DI WALCOTT
Well slightly embarrassed sir, DC Blaketon was tasked to complete the background checks, but no one seems to know where she is.

DCI CAMPBELL
I thought that I had made it crystal clear, she was only allowed back if she was kept on desk enquiries, I am not sure she is up to this and tracing and tracking Ann Jones is the only real lead we have, Reedy you do the checks and when Blaketon re-appears send her home… and that's an order… non-negotiable.

DI WALCOTT
One last thing Gov I've managed to track down the cadet training school Inspector, who was in charge of the class of 1981, a Katie Graham.

DCI Campbell looks blank.

DI WALCOTT
The class that had Jane Woodward the third victim and of course also contained Samantha Blaketon, which if I am honest Gov is not sitting comfortably with me, too much of a coincidence, Blaketon is somehow connected to our killer we know that and not just that he has decided to send her notes, think there may be more, so I thought the retired Inspector may be able to fill us in on her recruits and anything the initial investigation team may have missed?

DCI CAMPBELL
Another reason for her not to be here, OK go talk to the retired Inspector, let's see if there is more to this.

EXT: RETIRED POLICE INSPECTORS BUNGALOW - PRESENT - NIGHT

DI Walcott is outside of the bungalow with uniformed officers and a forensic crime scene team, blue lights and crime scene tape.

FORENSIC OFFICER
Yes, Inspector it would appear from what I have seen thus far to mirror the previous killings, large bladed kitchen knife MO is the same I would say as before knife to the stomach, but that comes with lots of caveats as we are only just processing the crime scene.

DI WALCOTT
OK Thanks, need to know about the victim and roughly when this happened?

FORENSIC OFFICER
Well remembering those caveats, I was just talking about… the victim appears to be retired police inspector Katie Graham. I'm pretty sure looking at the family and job photographs she has all over her bungalow, but as I say no formal identification carried out as yet. As for time very recent a few hours maybe no more, but I will know more when we have processed the whole scene and examined the body further.

DI WALCOTT
OK thanks keep me updated please.

DI Walcott pulls her mobile phone out and makes a call.

DI WALCOTT
Hi, it's me, major problem with talking to the retired police Inspector Katie Graham about her recruits and whether she knew an Ann Jones she's dead, ok it gets worse… she is also it would appear to be the latest victim of our killer. This is getting bloody weird and out of hand we need to stop this before he kills again.

INT: MAJOR CRIME POLICE OFFICE - PRESENT - DAY

DCI Campbell is leading an early morning briefing; DI Walcott and DS Reed are present along with other uniformed and plain clothes detectives.

DCI CAMPBELL

OK everyone, thanks for coming in early there has been another killing by, we think our killer although to be confirmed by forensics, plus some unusual developments about a potential missing witness or person of interest, but I will let DS Reed elaborate on that one. First DI Walcott will take us through the events of last night.

DI WALCOTT

Thanks, Gov, so we had identified former police training school Inspector Katie Graham as someone we needed to talk to about a potential person of interest who had not been spoken to around the initial killings… an Ann Jones. DS Reed will say more on Jones in a moment.

Before I could arrange contact with Katie at around 2115 hours last night her neighbour found her stabbed to death in her back garden. An early forensic view is that the MO is the same for our killer and this is his next victim. As usual no witnesses to the killing and not much forensics so far.

DETECTIVE
Ma'am is this Ann Jones a suspect?

DI WALCOTT
A very good question, it's complicated I think, DS Reed?

DS REED
Well where do I start… right then to re-cap what we know, for Vic one Nancy Williams and Vic two Fiona Harvey three friends including Sally Cameron, well Ann Jones was the fourth friend that was missed in the original investigation in 1979. But she was friends with the girls, only did not go out with them that night. It appears she was not interviewed at the time. If we jump to Vic four Hilary Todd, telesales supervisor killed in 1986, Ann Jones it has emerged worked at the same company and was in Hilary's team, again because she was off work when it happened the original team did not interview her. I know utter crap right.

DETECTIVE
Is she connected to Vic three then?

DS REED
I am getting to that, I initially thought no as Vic three was a police cadet, Jane Woodward murdered in 1981, however a deep search on Ann Jones has

revealed that she was actually born Samantha Ann Jones, date of birth 11 October 1962. According to the minimal amount of information I found she only appears on income tax data as Ann Jones... no police records, nothing with social services and virtually no health data.

However, I have found the most important bit of the puzzle that our Ann Jones, married in 1982. Anthony John Blaketon married Samantha Ann Jones at St Nicolas Church, the marriage only lasted two years before they divorced in 1985.

DCI CAMPBELL

Settle down, settle down yes you heard right DC Samantha Blaketon appears to be our Ann Jones, Blaketon is of course connected with victims one and two as one of their school friends and Vic three as she was a police cadet and on the same intake and course as Jane Woodward. We now know she worked with victim four Hilary Todd in the middle to late 80s. Safe to say people that Samantha Blaketon, current whereabouts unknown is now a person of significant interest in the investigation. We need to know what her connection to the killer is and why she has kept silent about her connections to the victims.

EXT: CREMATORIUM GARDEN OF REST - PAST 2018 - DAY

Samantha Blaketon is standing in front of some flowers that have 'Dad' on them, she is alone.

SAMANTHA
Don't worry Dad I know it was Mother that drove you to end your life, trust me one day God will take his revenge on that wicked witch.

A relative comes up and places a hand on her shoulder, they hug, speak, but it cannot be heard and the relative walks away.

SAMANTHA
And don't think I've forgotten that bitch Josie who broke your heart, she thinks she is untouchable now she has been elected as Commissioner but trust me Dad she will get what she deserves.

Blaketon's mother approaches and smiles at Sam.

And you can fuck right off.

Samantha walks off.

INT: MAJOR CRIME OFFICE - PRESENT - DAY

DI Walcott is sitting at her desk talking to DS Reed.

DI WALCOTT
Any update on Sam?

DS REED
Nothing, Ma'am, no sightings, not been back home, we have tracked her job mobile it's in her desk drawer. No one has seen her; I spoke to PC Ash yesterday who worked with her and is by all accounts her only real friend but has not seen her either.

DI Walcott's desk phone rings.

DI WALCOTT
Walcott, OK when did this happen… right thanks for letting us know, OK bye. Looks like Katie Graham may not be our killers only victim, that was the City Police last week an old lady was stabbed to death in one of their sheltered housing schemes, they thought it may be a robbery gone wrong so didn't flag it up to us, anyway they have now identified the woman
as Hilda May Jones… Sam's Mother.

DS REED
Fuck, we need to get hold of the Boss, she's our killer, has to be, forgotten witness my arse she has played us all and ducked and dived around the investigation over the years… now she's even managed to wangle herself on the main investigation team. Pretending to have been contacted and playing a potential victim…

another tactic to make us think the killer is male, I'll bet my pension on it. Just don't understand why?

DI WALCOTT
She is clearly out of control we need to find her before she kills someone else, maybe all this pretending to be a victim is some weird sort of plea for help or to be caught, who knows.

DCI Campbell comes into the office.

DI WALCOTT
Boss we think Sam's our killer.

DCI CAMPBELL
Miles ahead of you but hold that thought... Sam Blaketon has just walked into Ashton Street Police Station and handed herself in.

EXT: HOUSING ESTATE ALLEYWAY - PRESENT - EARLIER IN THE DAY

PC Matthew Ash is in plain clothes walking through an alleyway of a housing estate speaking on his police radio.

MATTHEW
Tango Kilo Five Seven to control I've checked the

area and there is no trace, over.

RADIO OPERATOR
Received Five Seven I will let the
informant know, over.

MATTHEW
All received as always, the kids causing the
ASB have long gone, Five Seven out.

He continues to walk back to his un-marked police vehicle when he notices someone sitting in the passenger seat, he looks hard then realises it is Samantha Blaketon. He smiles and gets in the car.

MATTHEW
Hello stranger, you checking up on me
now you're in major crime.

SAMANTHA
See you are as incompetent as always, leaving the
car unlocked and around here with those feral kids,
lucky the car is even here.

MATTHEW
See I'm lost without your guidance.

SAMANTHA
Look Matt I just wanted to see you and to talk to
you. As my lovely mother would have said if she

wasn't dead if we confess our sins, he is faithful and just and will forgive us our sins and purify us from all unrighteousness.

MATTHEW

Bloody hell Sam where did that come from what are you on about your mums dead?

SAMANTHA

Don't worry about that wicked bitch don't you see I am confessing my sins to you my lovely Matt… you have always treated me well and been a real friend to me and if it wasn't for all this perhaps we could have had even more.

MATTHEW

Look Sam I don't know what the fuck is going on, but you are freaking me out, stop talking religious rubbish, confessing to what…

SAMANTHA

Samantha pulls out a large knife.

Listen I love you Matt, but I'm going to have to ruin my life's work and take the life of such a sweet man so that I can finish all this and to ensure you will always be mine.

Matthew tries to half grab the knife and half defend himself, but Blaketon is too quick and stabs him in the neck. Blood spurts everywhere and Blaketon holds Ash while he dies.

INT: POLICE STATION FRONT DESK - PRESENT - DAY

Samantha walks into the front office of Ashton Street Police Station and goes up to the uniformed PSCO who is behind the enquiries counter. Samantha shows her police ID.

PCSO
Hello how can I help you?

SAMANTHA
Blaketon, Major Crime team, I am part of the kitchen knife killer task force did anyone let you know I was coming?

PCSO
Err oh no sorry no one has mentioned anything to me, who is it you need to see?

SAMANTHA
Don't worry, Detective Chief Inspector Andrew Campbell who is the senior investigating officer and who leads the task force has particularly asked me to come in today to see him. He said it was extremely urgent and vital to the investigation.

> **PCSO**
> Right, I see OK no problem I can let you in through the side door, but I am not sure where you need to go?

> **SAMANTHA**
> I will need an office or meeting room, as I have some urgent work to take care of, as I think the DCI is going to ask me to take a major lead in this high-profile case.

> **PCSO**
> OK. I better let the sergeant know then, he should be able to let you have a one of the side interview rooms for you to work.

> **SAMANTHA**
> Thank you, between you and me the DI is, shall we say punching above her weight on this case and out of her depth, so I think a promotion may be coming my way.

Samantha is buzzed into the police station by the PCSO.

INT: INTERVIEW ROOM POLICE STATION - PRESENT - DAY

Samantha Blaketon is sitting alone behind a table in an interview room. DI Walcott and DCI Campbell enter the room. Sam smiles at them.

> DCI CAMPBELL
> Hello Sam, you OK?
> Obviously, we seriously needed to talk
> to you about what is going on.

Blaketon sits smiling but says nothing, not looking at the officers.

> DI WALCOTT
> Look Sam you know why we need to talk to you…
> we know in the past you used part of
> your birth name… Ann Jones.
> We think that you know more about the kitchen
> knife killings don't you Sam. I am sure there are
> things you want to tell us, this all has to stop Sam.
> The notes emails the phoney threats. Think you may
> have even hurt yourself, Sam we need
> you to tell us everything.

> SAMANTHA
> Poor, poor Matty, loved that boy,
> no one else can have that man.

DCI Campbell gets up looking very worried and moves towards the door.

> DCI CAMPBELL
> Rights let's hold it there and take a short break we
> need to get organised and do this properly… I will

check on a solicitor for you Sam, then we can do this interview under caution. I'll also organise some coffee, DI Walcott will stay with you.

DCI Campbell leaves the interview room and speaks to a uniformed sergeant.

SERGEANT
All right sir, everything OK?

DCI CAMPBELL
Not sure, first can you speak to Major Crime and get them to check up on PC Matthew Ash who works in the community safety team, we need to just check he is ok. Second any chance we could organise some coffees, think this is going to be a long night?

SERGEANT
Yes, no problem sir, I'll get on to them straight away, oh and I will see what we can rustle up.

DCI CAMPBELL
Lovely thanks. Oh has a solicitor been organised for DC Blaketon?

                           SERGEANT
Err solicitor no sir didn't know she was under arrest,
she came in showed her police ID and said that she
worked in Major Crime and that the DCI, er you sir
wanted to see her urgently, so we just sat her in the
interview room out of the way so she could wait for
you. She said something weird though that she
                  was going to be your next DI?

The DCI starts running back to the interview room

                           SERGEANT
                      Is there a problem sir?

INT: POLICE INTERVIEW ROOM - PRESENT - DAY

Blaketon is still sitting at the table smiling, but has blood on her hands and top, a large kitchen knife lays on the table, covered in blood. DI Walcott is slumped on the chair, covered in blood and is dead. DCI Campbell and the sergeant rush into the interview room.

                          DCI CAMPBELL
                            Oh my God

Blaketon looks at DCI Campbell smiling.

SAMANTHA

God will not help you sir; I have learned that over my lifetime… just one more bitch who won't fuck with me again stopping me from getting on and another victim for the list… if you are counting.

END